Dear ? Johnson

Selected by
BILL ADLER

Illustrated by
CHARLES M. SCHULZ

ABOUT COMICS

These letters were selected in the mailroom of the White House during the winter of 1964.

They were chosen from the thousands sent each week to President Lyndon B. Johnson from American children.

I am most grateful to the efficient White House staff for their cooperation.

Bill Adler
New York City

Note: to maintain privacy, the names and addresses
of the correspondents have been altered.

Published by About Comics, Camarillo, California.
ISBN: 978-1936404-56-8
Send inquiries to questions@AboutComics.com

Dear President Johnson,

If there was a woman president would her husband be called "The First Man"?

Best wishes,
Mellissa F.
Indianapolis, Indiana

Dear President Johnson,

I am a Cub Scout in Indianapolis. Our finances are very low. We have 37 cents in our treasury. We need an American Flag to salute. We have been making our pledge to an old rug and pretending it was a flag at our den meetings. Could you send us one?

Yours,
Jimmy A.
Indianapolis, Indiana

Washington, D. C.
The White House

Dear President Johnson,

I, a future voter of this country, would like
to state my opinion on physical fitness in America.
I feel that you should set an example for the
people of America. Whenever you are shown on
TV, you are relaxing or taking it easy. This does
not make me get up and jump. I see the leader
of this country lounging around and
I want to lounge.

Sincerely,
Jack N.
Seattle, Washington

ONE, TWO, THREE, LOUNGE!
ONE, TWO, THREE, LOUNGE!

White House
Att: Mr. President

Dear Pres. Johnson,
    My mother and I heard you say on
TV that you cut the White House light bill.
My mother said, "Well, I'm not the only
person in the world who turns off the
lights." She is always turning off the
lights. Our house is always dark.

                    Your friend
                    Sarah G.
                    Los Angeles, California

Dear President Johnson,

Here is how you can win the election,

1. Promise a lot for everybody

2. Kiss all the babies

3. Be nice to dogs

4. Don't say too much that will get you in trouble

Good Luck,
Sally S.
Peoria, Illinois

Dear President Johnson,

I have been wondering about this for a long time. Why not have children act as foreign diplomats to other countries along with the older diplomats. I think kids would get more done over a game of checkers than the present older diplomats do arguing.

Yours truly,
Brian M.
Trenton, New Jersey

Lyndon B. Johnson
Washington

Dear Mr. President,

Our teacher, Miss Lang, gave the whole class a zero in spelling because a few boys were talking. She said "I don't care if you tell the President of the United States." So we are.

Sidney C.
St. Augustine, Florida

Deer Sur,
How kum I gott a
zeero in speling?

Dear President Johnson

I want to visit your LBJ ranch. I would like to be there for the Last roundup.

Your pal
John H.
Paterson, New Jersey

Washington, D.C.
Office of the President

Dear Mr President,
   I read in the Cleveland
Plain Dealer that you go
swimming without clothes
on. If you want to know my
opinion, I don't approve of
the matter, I think you better
start wearing a bathing suit
   Yours truly
   Ann B.
   Cleveland, Ohio

Dear President Johnson,

Do you know Huntley and Brinkley? You are always on their show.

So long,
Robert G.
Cincinnati, Ohio

OH, NO!
NOT
AGAIN!

The White House
Washington, D. C.

Dear President Johnson,

Our school is having Public Schools week.
I would like to invite you and Mrs. Johnson
to our school. If you can come I would like for
you and Mrs. Johnson to eat with me in the
lunch room. We eat at 12:15. My Mother will put
extra sandwiches in the lunch box for you and
Mrs. Johnson. I hope you like tuna fish.

Debra S.
San Francisco, California

SORRY...THESE TWO PLACES ARE RESERVED!

Dear President Johnson of THE USA,
  I am 11. I will be 12 next week.
How can I get federal aid?
  A girl from Chicago.
  Marsha R.

Dear President Johnson

I decided today to go to the local Democratic
club to obtain some pictures of you. I was
trying to combat the activities of a boy in
my class who was handing out republican li-
terature. Upon reaching the club, I found
that in a short span of time, it changed into
a Republican club. Republicans seem to be cl-
osing in on all sides. I can't find Democratic
headquarters anywhere.

Respectfu lly,

Tom H.

Milwaukee, Wisconsin

Dear President Johnson,

I would very truly like you to send me a hypnotism instructor to teach me how to hypnotize people.

The only reason I'm sending this letter is because there is this girl named Jennifer and I like her very much. I want to hypnotize her so she will like me.

Yours truly,
Dan B.
San Francisco

LIKE ME!
LIKE ME!
LIKE ME!
I CAN'T STAND YOU!

Dear Mr. President Johnson,

You probably don't remember me but on your visit to Florida, a red Ford pulled up next to your car and you were kind enough to open your window. I was the girl in that car.
I wish to apologize for seeming so rude to you and Mrs. Johnson. It's very hard to talk to the President of the United States. I mean, what is there to say? That is why I said nothing.

Love,
Harriet P.
Miami, Florida

Dear Mr. President,

What is your hobby? Mine is buying Monster Comic Books.

Love, Len W.
Boise, Idaho

Mr L.B. Johnson
Washington, D.C.
Dear President,
    I am a 12 year old boy and live
on the Grand Forks Air Force Base in
North Dakota. I have been sick with
colds ever since we have been here. I
wish we could be stationed somewhere
warmer. My daddy says we may be here
4 years. I think I would like Florida. I
have had 8 good colds already.
                Charles H.
        Grand Forks, North Dakota

To the President of the USA,

I would like to be the Senator from Wyoming in 1986. Please put my name on the waiting list.

Respectfully,
Mervin K.
Cheyenne, Wyoming

PROSPERITY
IN '86!

(1986, THAT IS)

Dear Mr. President,

    Your speeches are excellent except for one thing. You stop and look at your papers too much. If you would run thru your speeches
ahead of time, you would be a better speaker. Practice makes perfect.

                              Arnold J.
                              Lansing, Michigan

ADVICE FOR PRESIDENTS
5¢

PRESIDENT LYNDON JOHNSON
WHITE HOUSE

DEAR MR. PRESIDENT
     I READ IN A MAGAZINE
THAT YOU DRANK CAFFEIN
FREE COFFEE AND LOW CALORIE
ORANGE JUICE, IS IT TRUE?
WHY? YOU DON'T LOOK
FAT TO ME.
               YOUR FRIEND,
               PAUL H.
               CARSON CITY,
               NEVADA

President's White House
Washington
Dear President,

My name is Beth. I live in Boston. I have two brothers. No sisters. No dog. No cat. One turtle. I am in the fourth grade and I'm not married.

Bye,
Beth R.

Dear Mr. President Johnson,

     You never saw me and you probably never will. I wish I was in your shoes even if they wouldn't fit because then I would be more important than my brother.

Daniel S.
New Orleans, Louisiana

HOW
IMPORTANT
CAN YOU
GET ?

Dear Mr. President,

I am like you. I am President of our class.
I was elected by 12 kids out of 26. The other com-
petitors threw snowballs at me on the way home.
I thought that being a President was all
rosy. But it's not. How can you please everyone?
Can you help me?

A President,
Thomas P.
Albany, New York

P.S.   I will help you with your problems if I can

VOTE
FOR
ME

President L.B. Johnson
Washington, DC

Dear President Johnson,

                    I have one question
to ask. Our country broke away from ~~Englandxxx~~
England because of high taxes we had to pay.
But now we are worse off. The State of Indiana collects more taxes from the people than
any othere state. With all the taxes they
collect , Indiana should be richer than the
United States. Help the people of Indiana
before they don't have any money left.

                              Ellen J

Indianapolis, Indiana

DEAR PRESIDENT JOHNSON,

MY FATHER IS A SCHOOL TEACHER IN PALO ALTO. MY COUSIN DRIVES A BUS. MY BROTHER IS A COLLEGE STUDENT. MY UNCLE IS A DOCTOR. MY MOTHER IS JUST A HOUSEWIFE.

YOUR PAL,
JOE H.

President Lyndon Johnson
Washington

Dear President,

 If I could shake your hand, I wouldn't ask
for another thing for the rest of my life.

    Your friend,
    Stewart M.
    Hartford, Connecticut

EVEN FOR CHRISTMAS!

Dear President,

I am starting a hair collection. May I have some of your hair. I won't be disappointed if you need all your hair and you can't give me some. But please try hard.

**Love,
Jane T.
Denver, Colorado**

SIGH!

Dear President
Lyndon Johnson'
Please send your picture. I
want to have you in school.
Truly' Larry Z.
Springfield'
Massachusetts

The White House
Washington, D.C.

Dear Mr. President,

My friendsx and I are forming a club
in your honor. We call it the LBJ Young
Democratic club. We would like to have
a western hat or pins if you have any
to spare . And anything else to help
show that we are for you. The hat size of
my friend Jeffrey is 7 - Larry is 8 -
Richard is 7 $\frac{1}{2}$ - Andy is $7\frac{1}{4}$, Nicky is
$6\frac{1}{2}$ - mine is $7\frac{1}{4}$. The color hat we like
is white.

        THANK YOU,

            MARTIN K   Ann Arbor,
                              Michigan

Dear LBJ,

We are for you but against girls.

The Tiger Club
James R., President
Edwin B., Vice President
Alan C., Secretary
Ted J., Treasurer
Raleigh, North Carolina

EVEN CUTE
LITTLE GIRLS?

Dear Mr. Johnson,

My name is Bobby. I am nine years old. I am a cub scout. We have a 4 pocket scout salute but we can only do a 3 pocket salute because we can only do 4 if the President of the United States is at the meeting.

If you are around our town sometime I would like you to visit our cub scout meeting in our basement It's 6:30 on a Monday.

Sincerely,
Bobby T.

Mr. PresidENT
Washington, D.C.

Dear President Johnson,
    Is everybody in Texas tall like
You? Everybody in Vermont is short
like my father.

                    Goodbye,
                    Andrea W.

                    Burlington, Vermont

Dear Mr. President,

Do me a favor please. Sign my report card.
My Father won't.

Your friend,
Harold M.
Pittsburgh, Pennsylvania

LBJ

Dear President of the United States,

My name is Gretchen. I am 7 years old.
I want a horse. Is there a law against having a
horse in our garage?

Love,
Gretchen K.
Topeka, Kansas

THIS CAR IN HERE HAS COLD HUB CAPS!

Mr. Lyndon Johnson,
White House
Dear Mr. President,
    Our class is writing to
their favorite people. Most
of the kids picked the
Beatles but I picked you.
                    Love
                Helaine G.
        Fall River, Massachusetts

The President
Washington, DC

Dear President Johnson,

Our school year book has an ad section. We
would like you to buy an ad for the United States
Government. The prices are $36 for a full page,
½ is $24, ¼ is $12, 1/8 is $8. I hope the United
States Goverbment can afford a full page or at
least a half.

Thank you,

Earl P.

Twin Falls, Idaho

Dear Mr. Johnson,

Send to my house the number of boys in the country named Stanley.

My name is Stanley
Buffalo, New York

"STANLEY".... NOT "STANLIEGH"!

To Mr Lyndon Johnson
in the White House,
What does a President do
For Fun and Jokes?
Your friend.
Doug P.
Charlotte, North Carolina

Dear President Johnson,
 Our weekly reader had your picture with a Hereford Bull. We wonder what other animals you have on your ranch. What is your favorite breed of cat? We like like Siamese best. We have two cats in our howse but no bulls.

Your friend,
Lynn W.
Boston, Massachusetts

Lyndon Johnson
Washington

Dear Mr. President,

I hope we never have a lady President.
My reason is girls talk all the time. I know you
feel the same way but you can't say so because
you don't want to get the women mad at
you in an election.

Your friend,
Jeffrey W.
Seattle, Washington

VOTE FOR ME... I CAN DO ANYTHING YOU CAN DO !!

President Lyndon B. Johnson
The White House
Pennsylvania Ave.
Washington, D. C.

Dear Mr. Johnson,

I'm the girl you kissed in Houston. I am deeply honored to be kissed by the President of the U.S.A. I will remember it forever and ever.

Love,
Jeanine B.
Houston, Texas

P.S. Everybody knows you kissed me.

Dear Mr. Johnson,

I have a problem against parents. For example,
parents tell us we are noisy and then a few days
later they are laughing and yelling at night
and we can't sleep. If we tell them that they
are doing wrong we get in trouble again.

My two sisters and three cousins and I agreed
to call theis to your attention. Does a President help children out?

Schenectady, New York

PRESIDENT JOHNSON,
WASHINGTON
DEAR MR. PRESIDENT.

WON'T YOU GO TO OUR
CHURCH SOMETIME. OUR
CHURCH NEEDS THE
PUBLICITY. WE ARE
LUTHERANS.
                THANK YOU,
                RITA B.
BATON ROUGE, LOUISIANA

The President
The White House

Dear Johnson,

All I need is 18 cents to be the richest in
my class. Please.

Your pal,
Robert D.
Lansing, Michigan

P.S. MAKE IT 25¢
AND I'LL BE THE RICHEST
IN THE WORLD.

Dear Mr. President Johnson,

     I would like to know some real secrets.
I won't tell anybody. Not even my best
friend Harvey.

                    A loyal citizen,
                    Vincent J.
                    Providence, Rhode Island

Hi MR. PRESIDENT,
YOU NEED A SECRETARY FOR
CHILDREN IN THE CABINET
LIKE THE SECRETARY OF
AGRICULTURE BECAUSE CHILDREN
HAVE PROBLEMS LIKE
FARMERS DO.

THANKS,
MARCIA T.
LAS VEGAS, NEVADA

Dear President Johnson

You are probably wondering who I am? My name

is Betsy. I sent your name to the Peter Lewis

Store which sells Big and Tall man clothing. You will

no doubt receive a catalogue from this store. I

was wondering if you would place an order for

anything in the catalogue. I would receive a gift

for getting them a new customer. They have good

clothes and chaep prices. Thank you.

Betsy

New York City

Dear Mr. President,

I have seen you on TV a few times and I like the way you preach.

Janet T.
Denver, Colorado

AMEN!

The President
Washington
Dear Mr. Johnson,

The little boys and girls my age don't say much about most things but now we are. We do not think mailmen should shoot funny little guns at our dogs. Many times our dogs are blamed for things they don't do. Help the poor dogs, Mr. President.

Your friend,
Carole L.
Sacramento, California

U.S.
MAIL

Dear President Johnson,

We, the boys of the Junior Marines decided to
write to you about our Junior Marine Corps.
We know that a Marine is strong so we started
a gym in our basement. We have two nine pound
weights, one 27 pound weight, and one 18 lb.
weight. Each person takes five minute shifts.
~~Ixit~~ In five days we have become a lot stronger.
When we finish in the basement we trot around the
block once or twice. WE NEVER GET TIRED BECAUSE WE
ARE MARINES.

James S.

Dover, Delaware

President Johnson
Washington, D.C.

Dear Mr. President,
  Please write and tell me everything about your whole life. I need its for school. It can't be more than 100 words counting the title and by <u>Lyndon Johnson</u>.

                                   Best wishes,
                                   Marlys W.
                                   Bridgeport,
                                   Connecticut

Dear President Johnson,

If you were a little girl nine years old and you wanted to do something extra for your country what would you do? I only have a few afternoons off to help and I have to be home by five for my tub.

Love,
Beth T.
Stamford, Connecticut

ANOTHER DAY SHOT!

Dear President,

I am coming to Washington, D. C. on my
vacation. I would like to know if my dog, Rex,
can come to the White House. He has never been
to the White House. He will not bite and
he is not dirty. If it is okay can I come with him?

Your pal,
Leonard J.
Springfield, Massachusetts

WHITE
HOUSE
OR BUST!

White House
Washington, D.C.

Dear Mr. President,

My sister is running for President of the Hoffman School. We are trying the patriotic approach. Is that what you use? We are worried. Will it work?

Sincerely,
Leslie M.
Roslyn, New York

Dear President Johnson,

We are a 4th grade class in Chicago.
We are measuring distances around the tops of
our desks.
We use our hand span as the unit of meas-
uremnt.   Since the President is the most
important person in our country, we decided
we would use your hand xpx as our unit.
We will call it a "Johnson" and measure
our desks in "Johnsons".
We know you are a busy man, but could you
send us your hand span size?

Your friends: Barry A, David R., Stefan
               C., Dean L., X Jack Y.

Dear Mr. President Johnson,

Call me on the telephone. Here is my number, 311-555-2368. Don't call between 5 and 7 because that's when my sister is on the phone with her goofy friends.

Bye,
Richard S.
St. Louis, Missouri

SUDDENLY
I HAVE THE
FEELING IT
ISN'T GOING
TO RING...

Mr. Johnson
White House

Dear Mr. President,

I am starting a collection of famous marriage proposals. I need to have when you proposed to Mrs. Johnson and what you said. It doesn't have to be the exact words.

A loyal fan,
Eleanor K.
Bangor, Maine

P.S. If you forgot, ask Lady Bird.

WHAT IF SHE CAN'T REMEMBER EITHER?

Mr. President Johnson
The White House

Dear Mr. President
We are three brothers and
four sisters and my Mother
says thats enough.

So long,
Jasmine P.,
Portsmouth, Virginia

THE WHITE HOUSE
WASHINGTON, D.C.

Dear President Johnson,

I am one of your sincere followers, and I am
facing the long road of life for I am now a
teenager. I've got a distant dream to be a
lawyer and that is the reason I am writing
to you.

I wish you would send me one of your Texas
hats and then every time I am discouraged by
the hard work I'll have your "helping hat"
to give me courage when I need it most.

                    Thank you,

                    Edwin P.

          Abilene, Texas

Dear Mr. President,

I am eleven years old. My name is Mike.
Can you send me a Boy Scout cooking kit and ten
sleeping bags so my scout pack can go camping.
We are sleeping out in Jeffrey's backyard.

Thank you,
Mike T.
Harrisburg, Pennsylvania

Dear President Lyndon Johnson,

My name is Bobby Allen. My mother's maiden name was Johnson. My uncle checked back the records and found that you were my mother's sixth cousin and that makes you my seventh cousin. My problem is the kids in school don't believe me. Could you help me out since I am your seventh cousin for real.

Your seventh cousin
Bobby Allen
Houston, Texas

DEAR PRESIDENt JOHNSON,

I KNOW tHAt YOU ARE BUSY tHESE DAYS. I HAVE AN IDEA FOR YOUR COUNCIL ON PHYSICAL FItNESS MY IDEA IS tHAt IF YOU HAS A MR. & MRS. YOutH FItNESS PROGRAM, tHEY WOULD HAVE PHYSICAL GAMES.

BUD G.
SAN DIEGO, CALIFORNIA

Dear LBJ,

Would you grow a mustache for Timmy,
Annabel and my classmates?

Your pal,
Roger L.
Charleston, South Carolina

Dear President Johnson,
My friend, Freddy, said
that Mickey Mantle makes
more money than the President. It
isn't right. He just has
to hit home runs and you
have to watch Khruschev
and Castro

Victor S.
Salem.
Oregon

Notes for the 21st century reader:

Lyndon B. Johnson, often refered to as simply "LBJ," was the 36th President of the United States. While he had run for the position of being the Democratic candidate for President in the 1960 election, when the Democrats chose John F. Kennedy over him, Johnson accepted the vice presidential slot on the ticket, refering to his part of the Kennedy campaign as "the last roundup." When Kennedy was assassinated in 1963, Johnson become President, and then had a successful campaign for a second term in 1964. The President was known for his folksy rancher's style and his big Texas hats. His wife was commonly known as "**Lady Bird**."

Chet Huntley and **David Brinkley** were the anchors of the NBC evening news throughout the Johnson administration.

Mervin K. did not get to be Senator from Wyoming in 1986, as that state's two Senate seats were held at the time by Malcolm Wallop and Alan Simpson.

The Beatles were a popular rock band during the 1960s. While they disbanded in 1970, their work remains popular to this day.

Mickey Mantle was the first baseman for the New York Yankees at the time, and a record-setting hitter. **Nikita Khrushchev** was the Premier of the Soviet Union during Johnson's first term and **Fidel Castro** was Prime Minister of Cuba during the entire Johnson administration, both countries being seen as America's fiercest enemies.

The satirical New York Times best seller
returns to press for the first time in half a century

JFK
COLORING
BOOK

DON'T UNDERSTAND IT..THIS
AN INTELLECTUAL GAME... I
AN INTELLECTUAL ...AND
ET YOU ALWAYS BEAT ME!
I RE-RE-DOU
DOUBLE DOUBLE Y
DOUBLE DOUBL
ly a Game by CHARLES M. SCHULZ
ET ME WIN,
VE BEEN
ET ME WIN
OW IT
PPY TO
PPY!
I ALWAYS HATE TO SEE
HIM MISS A SPARE...HE
PUNISHES HIMSELF SO!
BONK!
BRIDGE
IF THE SPADE
FINESSE HAD WORKED
WE'D HAVE MADE IT!
I THINK I'M
GOING TO
CRY..
IT'S ONLY
A GAME
THE COMPLETE
COLOR COLLECTION
CHARLES M. SCHULZ
WITH JIM SASSEVILLE

96614201R00062

Made in the USA
Columbia, SC
03 June 2018